THE
BEER GURU'S
GUIDE

THE
BEER GURU'S
GUIDE

*Spiritual enlightenment
for those who thirst
for knowledge*

CHRIS STREET

SOUVENIR PRESS

Translated
from the original
Sanskrit tablets
found behind the tandoori oven
when the Balti Towers
Indian restaurant
was demolished.

"The capacity of beer to induce an altered state of consciousness makes it a powerful aid to spiritual development."

The Beer Guru

"Dedicated to the many enlightened souls who understand that drinking
beer can be a religious experience."

The Beer Guru

The Beer Guru's Teachings

1	The Beer Guru and The Barmy Swami	1
2	The Way of The Beer Guru	5
3	The Quest for The Holy Ale	9
4	Monks, Drunks and Holy Men	15
5	The Path of The Fool	21
6	Finding the beer equivalent of your soul mate	25
7	Brewing Your Own, The Alchemy of Ale	31
8	Dowsing For Beer	35
9	Creating Your Sacred Beer Space	39
10	Beer Shrines and Altars	45
11	Seeing Your Beer's Aura	49
12	Interpreting Your Beer's Aura	53
13	Blessing Your Beer	59
14	Initiation	63
15	The Initiation of The Whirling Pit	69
16	Opening Your Chakras	73
17	Becoming One With Your Beer	77
18	The Beer Goddess	81
19	Imaginary Ale Vs Real Ale	85
20	Tantric Beer Drinking	91

21	Mantras	95
22	Leys, Sacred Sites And Beer Lines	99
23	It's The Beer Talking	105
24	Invisible Friends	109
25	Reincarnation	113
26	Karma	117
27	Unlock the Secret Powers of Beer	121
28	The Mystic Properties of Beer	127
29	Out of The Body Experiences or Soul Travel	131
30	The Cave of the Beer Guru	137
31	The Dalai Llager and The Monastery of The Beer Brothers	141
32	The Beer Mat of The Holy Ale	147
33	The Temple of The Beer Goddess	153
34	The Font of All Wisdom	159
35	The Secret Of The Beer Guru's Smile	163

1

The Beer Guru and The Barmy Swami

The Beer Guru is a mysterious figure. Some believe he is part-man, part-god, a fully enlightened avatar who has incarnated on the Earth at this time to save humanity from its self-destructive tendencies and cheap canned lager.

Those who have seen him claim he is young and handsome, like Johnny Depp.

Others say he is a crazy old man with wild eyes and an unkempt grey beard which sprouts from his face like horse-hair from a burst cushion.

Both may be true, for in this life, we are all on a journey from youth to old age and beer can speed your transition dramatically, sometimes overnight.

It can also, if you follow the Beer Guru's teachings, be the font of eternal youth and wisdom.

As a young man, the Beer Guru trained for many years with a teacher and holy man, Sai Gaga, the Barmy Swami.

His teachings therefore stand on a long-established foundation of eastern mysticism.

His unique approach developed when it became time for the young Guru to find his own path.

He bade farewell to Sai Gaga and journeyed alone through the foothills of the Himalayas.

By a very circuitous route, his travels led him to Bavaria, where he met the renowned Braumeister, Otto Von Bonfire, who was destined to become his next teacher.

Otto was a direct descendant of the eccentric King Ludwig II, and was to entrust the young Beer Guru with the closely guarded secrets of the Bavarian brewers' art. (The Bavarian brewing purity law, the Reinheitsgebot, allows no artificial ingredients in their beers, making them the Beer Guru's equivalent of holy water.)

By the time he returned to his ancestral homelands, the spiritual knowledge of the east had fermented with the divine beer of the west and alchemically fused in the Beer Guru's mind.

He knew he was in a unique position to combine mysticism and beer in a heady potion.

In a secret valley, hidden high in the Himalayas, he created a sacred Beer and a new spiritual path.

A path of transformation and enlightenment through divine intoxication and the mysteries of beer.

The way of the Beer Guru.

"Beer is proof that there is a God."

The Beer Guru

The Way of the Beer Guru

When drinking beer,
there comes a point
where you are totally relaxed
and at one with the world
and all its people.

Where you feel
you are your true self.

At that moment,
the secrets of the universe
live in your heart
and you know all things,
past, present and future.

You taste eternity
and become as a god amongst men.

Yet the moment is fleeting,
like a dream.
It quickly fades.

Imagine
if you could hold that moment
and live within it
on an eternal wave
of blissful all-knowing.

That is the way of the Beer Guru
and all gurus.

If you are to experience it,
you must take the first step on the path.

You must undertake
The Quest for the Holy Ale.

"A journey of a thousand beers begins with a single bottle."

The Beer Guru

3

The Quest for the Holy Ale

High in the Himalayas lies the hidden valley of Shangri-La-La. In many ways it is a paradise. The climate is like summer, all year long. The women are beautiful and beer is more sacred than a stoup of holy water from Lourdes. There is no work, except the constant struggle for enlightenment, which can be achieved here by drinking the Beer Guru's divine fermentation, in one of the many beer temples, where one may also indulge in the more worldly pleasures of darts, cards, snooker, or watching football or cricket.

Beer temples abound. Glorious establishments, where the spiritually inclined may go at any time of day to sample the holy nectar and give thanks to the gods (and the Beer Guru) for providing it in abundance.

They are staffed exclusively by the impossibly alluring priestesses of the Beer Goddess, Kylie, who has far more arms than the average mortal female and so is perfectly equipped to fulfil her divine role as the bearer of the Holy Ale and Universal Provider.

The beer is known locally as Shangri-La-La-Lager, though it is as different to the average lager or beer as a diamond is from a lump of coal.

Shangri-La-La-Lager is the sacred beer created by the Beer Guru and revered by his followers. It is also the mythical Golden One, the Elixir of Life,

It does not give you a beer belly or brewer's droop. On the contrary, it promotes eternal youth, boosts sexual stamina, grants immortality and bestows infinite knowledge.

After one sip, you feel impossibly fit, strong, handsome and irresistible to all women. You become all-wise, all-knowing and can do anything you want to.

I realise, of course, that many men feel this way after a few beers of any sort. That is evidence of the mystical power inherent in all beer, though with the Golden One, the effects last longer than a few nano-seconds and you do not wake up the following morning feeling as if you have had a good kicking from the Russian ladies' shot-put squad.

The Golden One is the real thing. It is the Holy Ale. The Elixir of Life. It comes from The Font of All Wisdom in the Temple of the Beer Goddess, perched high on the cliffs overlooking Shangri-La-La's secret valley.

The only way into the valley is through the Monastery of the Beer Brothers.

The only way into the Monastery of the Beer Brothers is through the Cave of the Beer Guru.

The only way into the Cave of the Beer Guru is by Astral Travel.

There is no track or road. The only path is the path of the Beer Guru. You must follow his teachings religiously.

You must sample and study the best beers in the world, then learn how to unlock the secret power of beer and transmute it into your own sacred elixir.

This won't be as potent as the Golden One, but it will be your personal Holy Beer and will help you unlock your latent psychic powers, so that you can establish direct contact with your spiritual teacher, the Beer Guru and the monks of the monastery, the Beer Brothers.

With them as your spiritual guides, you will learn how to Astral Travel to Shangri-La-La, find the Temple of the Beer Goddess and drink from the Font of All Wisdom.

May your quest for the Holy Ale be successful.

May good fortune and the blessing of beer go with you on your spiritual journey.

"Some of the most lethal alcoholic drinks imaginable have been created by men of god, in places of spiritual reverence."

The Beer Guru

4

Monks, Drunks and Holy Men

Surprisingly, the Beer Guru is not the first to create an
unlikely combination of beer and spirituality. Holy Ale has a
long and illustrious history.

In the middle ages, the biggest brewers were
abbeys and monasteries.

"They are not drunks. They are holy men."

The Beer Guru

Nor did they limit themselves to beers. All manner of
wondrous wines, liqueurs and spirits were concocted by the
monks, who were allowed a generous daily ration for their
personal consumption.

Buckfast Abbey in South Devon, produces a brew so potent
that Glasgow's most hardened boozers revere it.

The Benedictine Order is responsible for a concoction
so potent it could render you insensible with alarming
rapidity were you unwise enough to consume it in
intemperate measures.

Abbott's Ale, The Bishop's Tipple, Augustinian Ale, Biere des Templiers and many other names on modern beer bottles bear witness to the fact that the history of beer is inextricably entwined with the great spiritual institutions of Europe.

Even the world's most famous beer festival, the Munich Oktoberfest, shares these religious roots. Munchen, as Munich is known in German, means the place of the monks.

Today's drinkers do not partake of these holy fermentations to bring themselves closer to an experience of the divine, but perhaps the original monks who brewed them did.

It is a well known fact that mystical experience is sometimes easier to come by when under by the influence of drink, or some other intoxicant.

"After just one bottle, I remembered several previous lives."

The Beer Guru

Many ancient cultures deliberately indulged in intoxication for enlightenment, or to induce an altered state of consciousness.

In Viking tradition, ceremonial drinking was known as Sumbel or Symbel and undertaken with great enthusiasm. Beer was consumed in vast quantities for inspiration and to promote the spontaneous recitation of poetry in the belief that it would encourage the words to flow as freely as the ale.

In the Mediterranean, initiates in the Eleusian Mysteries partook of a special ceremonial drink known as Kykeon, which played a large part in precipitating their visionary awakening or "epoptia".

These examples of ritual intoxication highlight the difference between everyday beer drinking and the path of enlightenment followed by the Beer Guru.

To the Beer Guru, drinking is part of a sacred ceremony a deeply spiritual experience undertaken with great reverence.

Not a bender.

"He who drinks beer, sleeps well. He who sleeps well cannot sin. He who cannot sin goes to heaven. Amen"

An old German monks' saying.

"You actually have to be
very well-balanced to tread
a path this crazy."

The Beer Guru

5
The Path of the Fool

When embarking on the way of the Beer Guru, be aware that
many will regard you as a fool, rather than a wise man.

This is true of any path of enlightenment,
not just this one.

"He's not a Guru. He's a piss-artist."

An unenlightened mortal.

When you take your first steps on a spiritual journey, you will
begin to see the world through different eyes.

You will have experiences that others would never imagine and
cannot comprehend unless they walk in your shoes.

Once you set foot on the way of the Beer Guru,
many things that you do, say or believe will seem like
madness to them. You will not be able to share your
experiences fully, for fear of ridicule.

For instance, you will not be able to speak to your Spiritual Guide, the Beer Guru in public. No-one else will be able to see him. People will think you are talking to yourself. They will suspect schizophrenia or drunken rambling, rather than a conversation with a wise and knowledgeable astral-travelling entity.

If you see a vision of the divine Beer Goddess, people will not immediately assume you are having a profoundly enlightening road-to-Damascus experience like St. Paul. They are more likely to think you are off your trolley.

In fact, some of the people you see in the street looking like drunks, talking to themselves, dancing with invisible partners and generally behaving very oddly may well be followers of the Beer Guru.

Though they appear to be suffering the symptoms of either complete and utter madness or total intoxication, they may, in fact, be experiencing the side effects of spiritual advancement.

As you can imagine, this is not a path for anyone who may be suffering similar symptoms already, so if you have a history of mental instability, emotional insecurity, anxiety, neurosis or alcoholism, The way of the Beer Guru is not for you.

On the other hand, if you don't take yourself too seriously and like a laugh, it probably is.

"The path of enlightenment
is strewn with empty
beer bottles."

The Beer Guru

6

Finding the Beer Equivalent of your Soul Mate

Before you can embark on the path of the Beer Guru, you will need to find a beer to use for your spiritual drinking exercises and to transmute into your personal Holy Ale. Any old beer will not do.

Bear in mind you will have to mingle your soul energies and life force with this beer. Its purity is of the utmost importance. Supermarket slop and cheap fizzy lager are not the gateway to higher realms.

"All beers are not the same. Some are heavenly. Some are diabolical."

The Beer Guru

The doors of perception can be opened only by those of the purest intent and for that, you must select the purest beer available.

Considerable research must go into this stage of the Beer Guru's quest, since you may have to travel extensively in search of rare and exotic beers, sample as many as possible, then decide which will be the beer equivalent of your soul-mate.

First, try the brews which conform to the Bavarian Purity law, the Reinheitsgebot, introduced by the Dukes of Bavaria in 1516, which decreed that only malted barley, yeast and water could be used to make beer, though hops are now permitted, too.

A pilgrimage to the Munich Oktoberfest, where most, if not all, of Bavaria's fine beers are available, should enable you to discern if any of these brews could be your personal nectar of the gods. However do not make a final choice until you have continued your pilgrimage and sampled the monastic beers of Belgium, France and England.

Particularly recommended are the vintage beers brewed by the Trappist Monks of Chimay in France, Biere des Templiers brewed in memory of the knights of old, Augustinian Ale from the Nethergate Brewery in England and King Cnut Ale from St. Peter's brewery.

King Cnut Ale is actually the closest match you will find to the early monastic beers of 1,000 years ago and it is brewed with nettles, not hops.

Savour as many of these beers as you can, until you find one that speaks to your heart and soul.

If this takes a considerable time, don't worry. Some followers of the Beer Guru remain at this stage of the spiritual quest for a great many years.

In fact, some never progress beyond it and presumably reincarnate to continue this worthy pursuit in their next life-time.

"In the beginning, god created beer."

The Beer Guru

7

Brewing Your Own: The Alchemy of Ale

The quest for the perfect beer leads many to learn the art of the braumeister. Indeed, some devote an entire lifetime to it, converting their sheds, lofts, garages, cellars and spare bedrooms into their personal home breweries.

Brewing your own beer shares much in common with the ancient art of Alchemy. Instead of transmuting lead into gold, you transmute water into the Golden One, your personal sacred beer.

Both acts are symbolic, for as you work at them, you unlock the secret powers of beer which can transform you, so that you become your higher self.

Your choice of water for the task is of utmost importance.

"Impure beer creates impure thoughts."

The Beer Guru

Beer for spiritual practices requires water from a holy well, not the stuff that comes out of a tap.

Malvern Spring Water would do (They have about 80 springs and wells to choose from) as would water from the Red Spring in Chalice Well Gardens at Glastonbury, from Holywell near Prestatyn in North Wales, from the well at the ancient St Mary's Church at Willesden Green in London, or from any of Britain's other holy wells. What you make your beer from after that is up to you.

Stick with the traditional hops, barley and yeast if you like. Or be more adventurous like the Belgian Trappists who brew beer with all manner of wondrous things.

You could even study druid herbal lore in depth and brew up something magical. Elderberry and Mugwort beer can be particularly eye-opening, in a psychic sense.

Beer made from magic mushrooms, though, is to be avoided. Its hallucinatory properties are devastating and sanity is notoriously difficult to restore once you've lost it. You only have one mind. Don't blow it.

It's quite likely that the hallucinatory effects of the earliest beers probably gave rise to the idea of magic potions. Under their influence, our ancestors may have imagined they could perform miracles, gain superhuman strength, see visions, visit other realms, be omnipotent, read minds, or understand the meaning of life.

Much like some of the people who drink beer today.

"After just one bottle,
I remembered several
previous lives."

The Beer Guru

8

Dowsing for Beer

There is not much difference between dowsing for water and dowsing for beer, except that you do not have to dig for beer.

All you need is a pair of L-shaped dowsing rods made from a couple of metal coat-hangers.

You can then walk into a supermarket or off-licence holding a dowsing rod in each hand and they will point instantly to the best beer in the place, thus saving you the trouble of reading lots of bottle labels and the expense of buying a large selection of beers to try.

Sceptics point out that the dowsing rods' swing, particularly when beer dowsing, could be explained by a person swaying gently from side to side.

This is a well-reported side-effect of beer, so it may well be part of the mysterious beer dowsing process, though under normal circumstances, the rods' reaction comes from minute muscle movements made by your subconscious mind, under the control of your higher self, which knows all things since it is part of the collective and universal consciousness.

Ignore any strange looks you get from other customers in the store. They are not as spiritually advanced as yourself and do not understand the actions of higher beings.

Be warned though, that the earlier chapter on the path of the fool is particularly relevant to the art of dowsing.

To the general public, there is a seriously high wally factor attached to walking around, holding a pair of bent coat-hangers.

"Nourish the inner man. Get a beer inside you."

The Beer Guru

9

Creating Your Sacred Beer Space

When you have selected or brewed your personal Sacred Beer, you must create a sacred space in your home where you can meditate, perform holy beer ceremonies, commune with the divine Beer Goddess and be open to inspiration from the creative forces of the universe.

Many ancient traditions utilise a sacred circle because it is a powerful symbol of the eternal circle of life and the infinite cycles of the heavens.

Followers of the Beer Guru must construct their own sacred beer circle. For this, you'll need a room with plenty of floor space.

Pour eight pints of your favourite beer and place them on the floor in a circle. In the centre of the circle, you'll need a cushion, or your favourite chair, where you can sit and perform your sacred beer rites.

Use a compass to make sure that four of the glasses accurately mark the cardinal points of North, South, East and West, to link your magic beer circle to the Earth's magnetic power grid. The other four glasses should be evenly spaced between them.

You now have a place of power, a beer temple plugged into the eight sacred directions. In terms of Feng Shui or geomancy, this is on a par with wiring up your beer to the cosmic mains. Placing your beers in this pattern empowers them with the universal and planetary life force.

Your first exercise within the sacred beer circle is to sit perfectly still. Try to attune to the power of universe now flowing through your beer.

This exercise will develop your ability to sense to the mystical powers that work through beer and utilise them for your personal benefit.

Resist the temptation to drink the beer, if at all possible.

This builds your strength of will and character for future trials on the path of the Beer Guru.

Failure in this latter part of the exercise is nothing to be ashamed of.

In all probability, you will drink a great many pints of beer before your will and dedication to the Beer Guru is strong enough to progress to the next spiritual level.

As you advance on the Beer Guru's path, you may wish to increase the power of your beer circle by creating more elaborate circles or even a beer henge such as those as used by the Druid Beer Brothers.

A sacred beer henge based on the great sarsens and bluestones of Stonehenge may require up to a hundred pints of holy ale and will be immensely effective as an open-air beer temple. It will also impress the neighbours.

"I drink, therefore I am."

The Beer Guru

10

Beer Shrines and Altars

"Beer is a sacred thing. Don't put it on a table, put it on an altar."

The Beer Guru

If you are serious about becoming a Beer Guru, you must also create an altar on which to keep your sacred beer.

Any small table will be suitable, if you cover it with a cloth of an uplifting colour. Royal blue, red or purple velvet will provide the perfect background for a bottle of the Golden One, though most followers of the Beer Guru seem to choose a football team's colours.

On the altar, you need to place the things you revere, things that inspire you, things that lift your spirits, speak to your heart.

Start with a bottle of your favourite beer, a bottle opener, a glass and a photograph of the first XI.

If you have any other spiritually uplifting items, or objects of devotion, feel free to use those too.

Some of the Beer Guru's followers like to display a photograph of the Dalai Llager, a small statue of "Our Lady of the Bottle Tops," or a picture of the Beer Goddess, Kylie.

Do not keep your cigarettes, crisps or darts on the altar. It would be inappropriate.

Remember, your altar is the focus of your special place of worship, your place of inspiration. It is therefore important that you place your altar in the correct location.

You won't need to consult a Feng Shui expert for this. Feng Shui practitioners are not Beer Gurus and have absolutely no comprehension of the sacred nature of beer, at all.

Place your beer altar in the centre of your sacred beer circle, next to your cushion or favourite chair, so that you can easily reach your beer when the Sacred Footie appears on TV.

"To start seeing auras, you need a couple of pints of Seers' Beer."

The Beer Guru

11

Seeing Your Beer's Aura

The phrase "seeing the light" is not without foundation.
When you begin to become aware of the spiritual dimensions
invisibly surrounding us, you do actually see the light, as a
halo or glow around people.

This is called an aura. Every living thing, without exception,
radiates an aura of spiritual energy. It is your life force. Your
soul energy.

Some people have a natural ability to see auras. Others can
learn. A few never see beyond the material world
and end up in politics.

Even beer has an aura.

You often see men in pubs holding their beer up to the light,
trying to see its aura.

For best results, place your bottle or glass against a plain
background. Sit comfortably in your beer circle and relax, by
taking long, slow, deep breaths. Slow your mind and still your
thoughts. Do not gaze directly at the beer. Look above it and
behind it so that the beer is slightly out of focus. You will then
see a fuzzy aura around it.

The more you drink, the easier it is to get things out of focus enough to see auras, so drink plenty of sacred beer to facilitate the experience.

In time and with enough beer and practice, you will begin to see a hazy glow around everything, beer included.

A word of caution. If you don't see an aura around your beer, you may be using the wrong one. Cheap canned lager has a very patchy broken aura, or no aura at all. It can be totally lacking in spirit or life-force. Do not drink it under any circumstances.

The Beer Guru brews a special Aura Ale known as Seers Beer, which bestows the power to see auras on anyone who drinks it.

After just one sip, you find yourself in a world where everything glows with a dazzlingly bright light, a bit like a washing-powder commercial but far worse.

You may emerge from the experience looking like a rabbit that has been caught in a car's headlights.

"Do not drink beer without an aura, it will drain your life-force."

The Beer Guru

"The quality of life is in direct proportion to the quality of your beer."

The Beer Guru

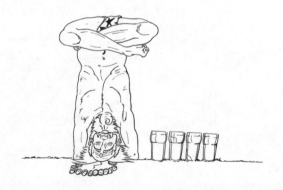

12

Interpreting your Beer's Aura

Generally speaking, the better the beer, the bigger and brighter it's aura. A strong, radiant aura means it is a beer suitable for spiritual use and sacred drinking.

When you have evolved your clairvoyance sufficiently to see the colours of an aura, you will notice that the purest beer has a rich golden hue surrounding it. This beer will be calming, will enhance mental faculties and improve the clarity of your thinking.

Very rarely, and only with spiritually enhanced beer, you might see a faint violet edge around the gold. This indicates that the beer's crown chakra is open and active. This is a beer in contact with its higher self and through which you can communicate with your higher being.

"Many cheap beers have an aura identical to the urine of a gnat."

The Beer Guru

Beer with a red tinged aura should be avoided as this can lead you to lose control of your temper, become uncharacteristically violent or abusive, or get involved in sordid sexual encounters with inappropriate partners. You may wake up in hospital, in jail, or in bed with a donkey.

Many spiritually un-evolved young men are attracted helplessly to this kind of beer.

Beer with a brown aura has a tendency to cause depression and leave you with a monumental headache.

Beer with bright patches of red and black, or with lightning-like flashes in its aura should be avoided at all costs. This is known universally as a Glaswegan Aura and can turn a quiet drink into a bar-room brawl in a split second.

A beer with a deep purple aura is potentially a magic potion and can enhance psychic abilities, induce past-life experiences or visions of the future. If its hallucinogenic properties are exceptionally high, you can find yourself spontaneously playing air guitar to seventies' heavy rock music no-one else can hear. Handle with care.

A beer with a deep blue aura will transform you into a moody bugger, though it worked well for Dylan Thomas.

A turquoise aura denotes a New Age beer. It will help put you in touch with your inner feminine and facilitate contact with extra-terrestrial beings from Sirius or disincarnate entities from the Pleiades.

You may begin to channel messages so deep and meaningful that they are totally incomprehensible to the average mortal, including yourself.

"Never drink anything that doesn't have a head."

The Beer Guru

"Your body is a temple. Always bless your beer and sanctify it before it enters your body."

The Beer Guru

13

Blessing Your Beer

Drinking beer is a sacred act, so blessing your beer consecrates it for spiritual use.

Mediaeval monks blessed their beer and marked the barrels with an X. They also used the same method to identify the strength of the beer since most monasteries brewed three strengths, X, XX, and XXX.

The best and strongest beer was for local dignitaries, important visitors and the elite of the abbey or monastery. XX was of average strength, for general consumption by the monks and their helpers.

The weakest beer, single X, was usually a cheap, watery ale for impoverished pilgrims, children and unsuspecting suckers.

The monks rarely brewed a four, five or six X beer since they were unusually harmful to the mental and physical well-being of the recipient. Their more positive benefits included their use as an early form of anaesthetic, where the X could also denote the number of teeth that could be extracted before the effect wore off.

Blessing your beer has the additional benefit of charging it with spiritual energy because the act of blessing changes the quality of the beer. It becomes as different from ordinary beer as holy water is from the stuff that comes out of a London tap (for proof if this, see the work of Dr Masuro Emoto).

The effect can also be observed by examining a beer's aura before and after blessing. In almost every instance, the blessing enhances and improves the beer's aura making it bigger and brighter. It also improves the beer's taste.

"A man with a beer is blessed. Therefore he should give thanks and bless his beer in return."

The Beer Guru

"The road of excess leads to the palace of wisdom."

The Beer Guru

14

Initiation

You do not begin a spiritual path without an initiation.

It marks the beginning of a new phase of your life, a new stage in your spiritual journey and path of self-transformation.

It is an act of commitment. An act of faith. An act of trust. A test. A threshold.

In the ancient mysteries, most initiations involved death and rebirth. Death of your old self. Birth of the new you.

To this end, the initiations often carried a very real risk of death or a near-death-experience, so that the initiate would return to this world (if they survived) with a valuable new perspective on the afterlife and a very real personal insight into the mysteries of the spiritual realms.

Being symbolically buried alive and rising from the grave to a new life is a feature of some Shamanic, Druidic and Masonic initiations.

The underworld initiation of the Western Mysteries requires the initiate to find his or her way through a dark cave alone. Here they will be confronted by their worst fears and the dark side of their inner self. They have to overcome their fears and faults to survive. Or not, as the case may be.

Christian Baptism, too, can be understood as an initiation based on a symbolic near-death by drowning. Survivors of drowning frequently report that their entire lives flash before them seconds before their expected death.

The initiation into the Egyptian mysteries of Osiris, which took place in the Great Pyramid, involved being drugged and bound like a mummy, placed in the sarcophagus in the King's chamber and left there in the dark for several days. The initiate either learnt how to get out of his body and astral-travel, or he died of fright and got out of his body permanently.

According to the Beer Guru, initiation into the mysteries of beer can often be just as challenging.

Predictably, it features a beer-induced near-death experience during which the initiate may really think he is going to die. This inevitably involves drinking enough to pass into a state of altered consciousness where the initiate experiences nightmarish dreams and visions of hell. He awakens to find himself in a remote location, feeling as if he is at death's door, covered in vomit and with no idea how he got there. When he begins to recover, he may feel that he is still going to die, in a most painful manner. He will swear he will never drink again. Ever.

This really is a valuable lesson. A real life and death test is involved. Every time you get wasted on booze, approximately 100,000 brain cells die and are never replaced.

If you have drunk more than your body can physically cope with, you could actually die of alcoholic poisoning. Or choke on your own vomit like a drummer in a rock band. The very least you will suffer is a throbbing head and a technicolour yawn.

If you have survived such an initiation and are a wiser person for it, you are ready to tread the path of the Beer Guru.

Learn from your mistakes. If you do not, you are heading for the abyss of the whirling pit.

"If you are lying on the pavement and have to hold on, you are out of harmony with the celestial movements of your Mother, the Earth."

The Beer Guru

15

The Initiation of the Whirling Pit

The Earth turns once every 24 hours. Its surface speed is over 1,000 miles per hour. It hurtles through space at 66,000 mph.

We don't normally feel this movement at all, because we are an intrinsic part of our mother planet. We move as one with our world.

Excessive beer consumption can dislocate the harmony of this relationship.

It puts our chakras so out of balance that we become out of synch with the spin of the polar axis. We cannot stand and we cling to the ground for fear of being hurtled off into space.

Our psychic channels are torn open and instead of revealing the higher spiritual realms, they open a yawning chasm beneath us to Hades and the black, bottomless bowels of the Earth.

When people have a near-death experience, they report going down a tunnel towards the light. The whirling black pit is what lies in the opposite direction.

"It reminded me of a previous life as a spin dryer."

The Beer Guru

There is heaven and there is the other place. This is the other place. You don't want to go there.

It is a hideous realm ruled by the Lord of the Whirling Abyss, a drink demon who takes the form of a giant, pink elephant.

Always maintain your sacred beer intake at a level which will not precipitate a vision of the whirling pit.

"It is easy to tell if your chakras need balancing. You fall over."

The Beer Guru

It's easy to tell if your chakras
need balancing. You fall over.

16

Opening Your Chakras

Many eastern mystics and new age psychics insist that you must familiarise yourself with the concept of opening and closing your Chakras before you can evolve spiritually.

Chakras are spiritual energy centres in your aura. Most people can't see them and don't have a clue about where or what they are.

If your personal knowledge of them is similarly lacking, you will be relieved to learn that an in-depth familiarity with them is not a pre-requisite for those following the path of the Beer Guru.

All you need to know about chakras is that to open a beer's crown chakra, you need a bottle opener.

"Never open your chakras when you have been drinking. Your brains will fall out."

The Beer Guru

"We live in a holistic universe. Beer can connect you to the source of all creation."

The Beer Guru

17

Becoming One with Your Beer

By now, you should have created a sacred beer altar, set up a sacred beer circle, survived the initiation of the whirling pit and started to see your beer's aura. It is time to move on to the next stage of the Beer Guru's teachings and start to unlock the secret power of beer.

All things are connected. You must now learn some of the connections.

We live in a holistic universe where all things contain the essence of the whole. The secrets of the universe are in all things, especially beer.

"All things are connected spiritually. Especially men and beer."

The Beer Guru

To merge with the unity of the universal life force and know all things, you must become one with it. To do this, you must drink sparingly, barely a sip of your beer, until you reach that peak moment when illusion melts away and you feel at one with the universe.

Seize the moment. It is fleeting, but feel it, hold it, for it contains eternity.

Within this peak beer moment is the eternal you, that lived before your birth and will live on after your apparent death in this world.

It is the magic of the Beer Guru's way that you can come to know your immortal higher self in these flashes of beer-induced self -knowledge.

This may take weeks, months or years of dedicated practice. Persevere. Remember. In this instance, the less you drink, the longer you may hold the eternal moment.

"Less is more."

The Beer Guru

"If god is omnipresent, he is in your beer."

The Beer Guru

18

The Beer Goddess

Now it is time to discover exactly which aspect of divinity resides within your pint pot. The Beer Guru's beliefs are very clear on this, but totally at odds with mainstream religion. According to him, the aspect of divinity present in beer is feminine, the Beer Goddess.

As you work with the previous exercise to become one with your beer, you will catch fleeting visions of her.

She will appear to be your perfect woman.
Knowledgeable and wise.

She will fill your heart and soul with love, because she is caring and understanding.

She will bring you as much beer as you want, because she is the Universal Provider.

She may even want to have astral sex with you as you meditate in your sacred beer circle.

Sceptics will say that she is simply a booze-induced fantasy.

As a devotee of the Beer Guru, you will find she is your soul-mate from an alternative spiritual reality.

However, we must offer a word of warning. Do not confuse visions of the Beer Goddess with the phenomenon of Beer Goggles.

Beer has the ability to make members of the opposite sex appear far more attractive than they really are. Hence the idea that you are viewing them through the miracle of Beer Goggles.

The more you drink, the more attractive they become. Until you reach the point where every female you see appears to be impossibly beautiful, the Beer Goddess incarnate and the woman of your wildest dreams.

"Through the miracle of beer goggles, you can see the inner beauty of anyone."

The Beer Guru

If this happens, you will be in big trouble. Because when the beer goggles' effect wears off, the object of your desire will revert to her ordinary, normal self and the attraction will disappear as if you had been under some kind of enchantment (which you were).

It is an example of the dark side of beer's spiritual powers.

Do not be tempted by the dark side. Darth Vader cannot drink a single pint with that silly helmet on.

"Everything is maya, illusion.
Even real ale. Imaginary ale ought
to taste just as good."

The Beer Guru

19

Imaginary Ale Vs Real Ale

(A Beer Guru Meditation)

According to many mystical traditions, what we generally call the real world is maya, illusion. Life is but a dream. And we are the dreamers. Even scientists know that our reality is an illusion. Quantum physics tells us that every solid object you see is actually 99.99% nothing.

What we see as solid objects are sub-atomic particles whizzing about so much that they are a blur of activity creating the illusion of the material world. And even they cannot be wholly described as solid since they may become wave phenomena at any moment, unpredictable little blighters.

The terrible conclusion we have to draw from this is that even Real Ale is not really real.

I realise this will come as a dreadful shock, but it does have a positive side. It means that when you don't have a real beer, you can have an imaginary one and, theoretically, it will taste over 99% as good as the real thing.

Of course, you would have to drink it in a form of Beer Guru Meditation.

The Beer Guru has no truck with meditations that require a superhuman act of will to empty the mind. He knows your mind is mostly empty already, except for sex, football and beer.

What you need to do is fill it up with Imaginary Ale.

Sit in your sacred beer circle. Meditate on the beer upon your altar. Visualise yourself pouring that beer into a glass. In your imagination, lift the beer to your lips and savour every drop.

Imagine you can smell its aroma. Imagine you can feel the cool, sparkling liquid tantalisingly trickling over your taste buds.

Imagine you can feel it bursting refreshingly on your palate.

Imagine swallowing that first wonderful mouthful. Imagine the glow of pleasure it spreads throughout your body.

Imagine relaxing into a deep state of bliss, where you feel deep peace and are at one with God and the universe.

Remember, on the higher spiritual levels where your meditation reaches, your Imaginary Ale is as real as Real Ale and it has the power to awaken your latent super-human potential.

Exercises such as this are designed to stimulate your inner vision, your imagination, your clairvoyance.

You can tell it is starting to work, when you begin to feel a little drunk.

The great beauty of drinking Imaginary Ale is that it doesn't cost a penny. It can save you a fortune in the pub on a Friday night.

"Getting drunk on imaginary ale is to enjoy the other-worldly delights of transcendental intoxication."

The Beer Guru

"After eighteen hours of Tantric
sex, I need a beer."

The Beer Guru

20

Tantric Beer Drinking

The stories you hear about Tantric Beer drinking are true. You can keep it up for hours and hours. It takes some practice, but the results are well worth the effort.

The first stage involves aligning your chakras to those of the beer and creating a harmonic resonance between beer and self. This is part of the advanced process of becoming one with your beer.

Don't actually drink the beer. Just absorb its vibrational essence. At the same time, shift the energy from your physical beer-drinking chakras, the throat and belly, and move it to the higher spiritual chakras of the heart and mind.

This is done through a combination of pelvic floor exercises and synchronised breathing which squirts the energy up the nadis (Kundalini pathways) to the higher centres.

In terms of spiritual energy, it's all about getting it up and keeping it up.

"If you're having a drink prior to tantric sex, make sure it's a stiff one."

The Beer Guru

"Om shandy.
Om shandy.
Om shandy."

A Beer Guru Mantra

21

Mantras

Mantras are phrases which you repeat to induce a semi-hypnotic state of transcendental meditation in which you can lose your sense of self and become one with your beer and the universe.

The most well known Mantra is "Om", the Sanskrit word for the sound of creation. Its Sanskrit symbol is written like a number 3 with an extra loop attached at the back.

The Bible says that in the beginning was the word. If there actually was a word in the beginning, it was "Om". Or something very like it.

Chanting "Om" creates a harmonic resonance between yourself and the creative forces of the universe, so that you become your own power centre.

As you chant, healing, regenerative energy is carried out from you on the waves of sound. You become a ripple in the pond of the life-force and life-enhancing energy flows from you to re-attune the world around you to the greater harmony of the celestial realms.

It is said that chanting "Om" 1,000 times in a deep and meaningful way, purifies you so well that you could drink several bottles of Druid Fluid (an extremely strong and intoxicating brew) with no harmful effects, though I wouldn't personally put it to the test.

The next best known mantra is "Om mani padme hum" a Tibetan prayer mantra which means something like; " Om. Salutations to the jewel of consciousness which has reached the heart of the lotus. "

The Beer Guru has a similar mantra: "Om mandy patme bum." Religious scholars say it has no direct meaningful translation, since it by-passes the limitations of verbal communication and speaks directly to the soul.

As a devotee of the Beer Guru, you will find that you by-pass the limitations of verbal communication frequently.

Take this as a reassuring sign that beer and mantras can combine powerfully to create altered states of consciousness.

In view of this, beginners on the Beer Guru's path might like to start with the simple chant: "Om shandy. Om shandy. Om shandy."

More experienced students can try the Beer Guru's favourite mantra: "Om onlee avin naquik wan."

Repeat endlessly until transcendence is achieved.

"Pubs have their own ley lines. The centre of the network is The Red Lion, in the middle of Europe's biggest stone circle, Avebury."

The Beer Guru

22

Leys, Sacred Sites and Beer Lines

Since the publication of Alfred Watkins' book, *The Old Straight Track*, in 1925, it has been known that pre-reformation churches, standing stones, holy wells and other ancient sacred sites formed linear patterns on the landscape, now known as leys.

To the academic world, leys are a questionable phenomenon, a source of constant controversy.

To the mystic, they are no enigma. They are pathways of the planetary life-force, the Earth Spirit, which often manifests as an apparition of a goddess or white lady at significant nodal points along their length. Such apparitions, it is believed, gave rise to the sacred places which mark leys.

Shortly after the publication of *The Old Straight Track*, a second, less-well known book came out, dealing with a related phenomenon. It was Wilfred Atkins's book, *The Wibbly Wobbly Way*.

Atkins had noticed that some leys not only included monasteries, abbeys and other sacred sites where beer is brewed, but ancient public houses where it is consumed.

He suggested that Britain's pubs have their own
ley system of Beer Lines.

Its centre is at Avebury Henge, Europe's largest megalithic
stone circle. Or to be more precise, at The Red Lion, which
stands at the centre of the circle.

Radiating out from here is a network of Beer Leys linking
pubs across the length and breadth of the land.

If this is correct, our oldest pubs were built upon ancient
sacred places along the leys. They are power-points in the
world grid where we can plug into the cosmic mains and our
spiritual source. The Beer Leys which link them form part of
the sacred landscape of Britain.

Beer Leys are not straight like Alfred Watkins' leys. They
meander wonkily across the landscape from pub to pub,
like a drunk on a night out. Atkins was quick to point out
that this perfectly represents the influence of beer on the
ley line system.

However, it also mirrors the findings of experienced dowsers
who have made a lengthy investigation of Britain's longest
alignment; The St Michael line, which runs right across the
country linking a line of St Michael's churches from St
Michael's Mount in Cornwall to Norfolk.

They discovered that the St Michael line actually contains two dowsable energy polarities which weave and meander around each other in exactly the same way as Wilf's Beer Lines.

Incidentally, the Michael line crosses one of Wilf's lines at Avebury. The exact spot is marked by a huge stone with a seat carved into it.

It is a great place to carry a beer from The Red Lion as the stone faces the mid-day sun at its zenith and can be a very empowering place to sit (please remember to take your beer glass back to the pub afterwards).

Dowsers have much success in tracing these energy lines, so it is worth learning their techniques to find the most powerful places to attune to your beer. Beer energy nodes.

If you have developed a degree of sensitivity, you will feel the energy of beer lines as a distinctly wobbly sensation as if you have just had a bottle of Stoudt's Abbey Triple (9%) on an empty stomach.

When you find a really strong power point, you may suddenly find yourself incapable of standing and be caught up in a swirling vortex of energy that throws you to the ground.

Once you have identified a suitable spot, remain spread-eagled on the ground like a starfish and attune to it. Ignore passing comments like; "Earth-hugger" or "piss-artist".

Lie there until the dizziness wears off, then you can connect to the Earth's power pulse and expand your consciousness to that of the planet.

When you are at one with the planet, your aura will be roughly 25,000 miles in diameter.

You will have grown in spiritual stature accordingly.

"Drink me. Drink me. Drink me."

The Beer Guru's Beer speaking to him.

23

It's the Beer Talking

There will come a point in your training as a Beer Guru when your beer will begin to speak to you. Do not be alarmed. It is the still, inner voice that we normally cannot hear above the clamour of our own thoughts.

Opinions vary on who or what the voice represents. Some think it may be the voice of your higher self. Others are convinced it is the voice of God. Followers of the Beer Guru are more likely to hear the voice of the Beer Goddess, or the Beer Bhudda.

Listen carefully and keep notes. You never know, it might tell you the winning numbers for the national lottery.

More likely it will give you spiritual advice or teach you something about beer that no earthly person could ever have known.

If, however, it tells you to hack people to pieces with a chainsaw, something may be amiss. Do not listen.

A related phenomenon is channelling. This is when a spiritual entity uses the medium of beer to enter you and speak through you.

Whether this is a good thing or not depends on who the entity is and what it wants.

If it is the Beer Guru, the Beer Goddess or one of your other spirit guides, all well and good. You will be the life and soul of the pub, speaking reams of wisdom and telling hilarious jokes.

As a general principle though, channelling is not recommended for beginners. You could attract a spook who has been hanging around the bar looking for a likely victim to move into. Watch out for the warning signs;

If you suddenly start speaking in a funny voice, in an unusual accent or in an incomprehensible language, or if you begin to make uncharacteristically abusive comments, suspect that you have been possessed temporarily by a beery entity.

Get a grip. Apologise profusely and explain that it was just the beer talking. Even the most unspiritual people will understand.

However, you must go and get yourself exorcised as soon as possible, particularly if your head rotates through 360 degrees and you begin projectile vomiting.

"Life's short. Drink as much as you can."

The Beer Guru

24

Invisible Friends

As you work with your Sacred Beer and the Beer Guru, you will begin to evolve into a wiser being yourself. Your psychic Third Eye chakra, will activate and make denizens of the spiritual realms visible to the naked eye.

In the privacy of your Beer Sanctuary, or Sacred Beer Circle, this will be no problem.

However, there is nothing more disconcerting than to have Tonto, your American Indian spirit guide, trying to attract your attention when you are in the pub with your non-spiritual mates.

Some of your friends will accept your new eccentricities. Others will look at you like a rabid dog and take a wary step backwards.

Invisible friends are fine when you are a kid. Everyone puts it down to an active imagination. If you have them when you are grown up, the men in white coats may come and give you a syringe full of stupefying drugs and a nice jacket that laces up at the back. You don't want that.

The Beer Guru recommends talking to your spirit helpers in private and asking them nicely not to bother you when you are going about your daily affairs.

While we're on the subject of invisible friends, whatever else you do, do not hook up with an invisible girl friend. It will be a relationship plagued with problems.

I know you will meet some wonderfully attractive Beer Angels and Priestesses of the Beer Goddess as you travel the path of The Beer Guru, but they are not human and cannot be like normal girlfriends.

They are mythical creatures who exist on a higher dimensional plane. If you fall in love with one, no one else will be able to see her.

On the plus side, this means that none of your mates will try to hump her behind your back.

On the downside, when the temptation for you to snog her head off in public becomes too much, those who can't see her will be wondering what on earth you are doing with your tongue.

"Reincarnate and come back for another one."

The Beer Guru

25

Reincarnation

The cycle of life, death and re-birth is eternal and natural.
Night follows day. Day follows night. Beer follows beer.

It is the way of all life and of our spiritual evolution.

**"Not all previous lives are as Pharaohs or High
Priests. In one, I was a Neanderthal pot man at
the Sir Richard Steele pub in Belsize Park."**

The Beer Guru

As an acolyte of the Beer Guru, you are evolving beyond the
limitations of a single human lifetime.

When you die next time, your immortal soul will be
reborn in a new life to continue your pursuit of
enlightenment through beer.

The Ancient Egyptians had such faith in life after death they
left beer in tombs for the deceased to drink in the afterlife.

The Druids were so convinced of the immortality of the eternal soul, they frequently borrowed money and arranged to repay it in the next life. Sadly, you can't get away with that one these days.

However, it is a reassuring thought for many that, unlike money, beer can be taken with you when you die.

All you have to do is drink as much as you can, just before you go.

"A monster hangover is a perfect example of karma, the spiritual law of cause and effect."

The Beer Guru

26

Karma

Karma is the universal law of cause and effect. For every event or action that occurs, there will follow another event whose existence was caused by the first.

This second event will be pleasant or unpleasant depending on whether the first event incurs good or bad Karma. Therefore, the law of Karma teaches that the responsibility for any action is borne, in this life or the next, by the person who commits it.

Karma operates over such a vast timescale that there is no point in attempting to work out whether you are repaying Karma or incurring new debts or credits. It would be wise, therefore, to always assume that you can usefully notch up some good Karma.

Do good, be kind, generous and compassionate to all you meet. Leave them thinking the world is a better place for having you in it.

"If someone buys you a beer, get them one in return. You do not want to run up a karmic beer debt."

The Beer Guru

"After a couple of beers, you love everyone and everyone loves you. Beer is liquid love."

The Beer Guru

27

Unlock of The Secret Powers of Beer

In Lesson nine, you created your sacred beer circle. By now, you should have spent many happy hours in it attuning to the mysterious and miraculous forces that flow through beer.

Now, it is time to learn more of the Beer Guru's art and use those forces to unlock some of the secret powers of beer.

To do this, you need to work in your sacred beer circle of eight pints, in order to connect yourself and your beer to the power of the Universal Life Force.

Sit at the centre holding a ninth beer. This ninth beer represents the magical one-over-the-eight and creates an Axis Mundi, literally an axis of power through the centre of your circle, linking you and your beer to the life-force of the stars above and the Earth below.

Breathe slowly, deeply and gently. Relax and on each breath breathe out all your tension, all your cares. Then visualise a column of light shining down on you from above. A column of light which comes from the centre of the universe.

"With just the beer light to guide us."

Ziggy Stardust and the Spiders from Mars.

As you breathe in, breathe in the light. Breathe it into your body, your head, your chest, your arms, your stomach.

More important, breathe the light into your beer, first into your central ninth pint, then radiating out into the other eight, so that eventually you feel that your entire sacred beer circle is engulfed in light and power.

At the same time, let the love you feel for your beer go from you into the glasses. Love your beer unconditionally. Fill your beer with light and love, man.

"Love is beer. Beer is love."

The Beer Guru

Do this exercise for as long as you feel necessary, until you and your beer are totally energised and empowered by the universal life force and are glowing with golden light.

Enjoy the sensation of power and well-being.

You have now created nine pints of Light Ale, your personal version of the Golden One, charged with the secret powers of beer.

Be wary of its power.

Many beers bestow the illusion of immortality and eternal youth.

After only a few pints of anything, old men feel young again, dance with renewed vigour, imagine they are attractive to women young enough to be their daughters.

Young men become fearless and imbued with super-human powers and imaginary immortality.

Sadly, the effect usually wears off rather quickly and they awaken the next day, looking a lot older and world-weary, to remind them of their mortality.

The Light Ale you now possess is different. Do not waste it by guzzling it down. Savour every drop spiritually.

You will find that beer energised by the life force will taste quite different and be far more beneficial.

It may even refresh the parts that other beers cannot reach.

"Just one pint of spiritually charged Light Ale enables you to hear the sound of one hand clapping."

The Beer Guru

> "

"The key to the mysteries."

The Beer Guru

28

The Mystic Properties of Beer

Now you have nine pints of your personal Sacred Beer,
your own Light Ale.

It is not so potent as the fabled Shangri-La-La-Lager, the
Golden One, so you will not yet be all-knowing, all-wise.
Nevertheless, Light Ale possesses mystical powers which can
work miracles for you. Here's a short list of what it can do.

It can give you super-human strength.
It can give you amazing self-confidence.
It can grant you immortality.
It can make you invincible.
It can make you impervious to pain.
It can give you boundless energy.
It can make you a wonderful conversationalist
and raconteur.
It can make you a terrific poet.
And a great karaoke singer.
It can give you faultless dress-sense.
It can make you impossibly attractive to the opposite sex,
irresistible to all women.
It can give you a bigger willy.
It can give you psychic powers.
It can make you telepathic.
It can help you astral travel

for out-of-the-body experiences.
It can give you a vast sexual appetite
for in-and-out-of -the-body experiences.
You can belch and fart as loud as you like
and no one will notice.
Not even you.

"When you learn to astral travel, you will find there are far more interesting places to go than the local pub."

The Beer Guru

"When you learn to astral travel,
you will find there are far more
interesting places to go than the
local pub."

29

Out of the Body Experiences or Soul Travel

**"To get out of your body, you
first have to get out of your head."**

The Beer Guru

Since you have now learned how to plug yourself into the cosmic mains and have activated your light body and created your miraculous Light Ale, you can now learn to astral travel.

It is the only way to get to the Cave of the Beer Guru, the Monastery of the Beer Brothers, the Temple of the Beer Goddess and the Font of All Wisdom.

The big question is: how do you do it?

The answer is simple. With the nine pints of cosmically charged Light Ale you've just made. One pint will be enough to get you completely out of your head and then your mind can go anywhere it likes.

It is free to travel along the Beer Leys to the eight corners of the universe, to any world, to any dimension, to any realm, to the past, to present or future. Even to places that don't actually exist: the worlds of Hobbits and Elves or Harry Potter.

Where your mind goes, your consciousness goes, a spark of your soul goes.

"Think of me as your Astral Travel Agent."

The Beer Guru

How about a trip to the centre of the sun? Or to Machu Pichu and back in an afternoon? Or to the lost city of Atlantis? Or into the bedroom of the gorgeous barmaid from the Rose and Crown?

Thomas Cook doesn't do those kind of trips, but you can if you learn to astral-travel.

Do not drink more than one pint per trip. Too much Light Ale facilitates astral travel, but impairs the memory, so you can't remember where you have been or what you have been doing. Not much point in going anywhere under those circumstances.

The Beer Guru has found that one of the best ways to get out of his body is to visit a lap-dancing club, where he passes into an almost trance-like state staring at the girls. This helps the process of getting out of his head, so he can leave his body there for a couple of hours.

In the distracting surroundings of Spearmint Rhino or its sister club, Peppermint Hippo, no one would ever think the glazed eyes and mesmerised grin were anything out of the ordinary.

The only problem is that sometimes he comes back and finds that his body has mysteriously run up a sizeable bar bill and has stuck most of his money down the lap-dancers' knickers.

Like everything else, soul travel takes practice. Put aside a couple of hours a week to take yourself on a trip.

With a little practice, you will soon be ready to undertake journeys to the Cave of the Beer Guru, the Monastery of the Beer Brothers and the Hidden Valley of Shangri-La-La.

"Beer is a portal to other dimensions."

The Beer Guru

30

The Cave of the Beer Guru

When you have become a regular astral traveller and have been granted a passport to metaphysical drinking realities, you may travel to the Cave of the Beer Guru.

The journey will begin with the Beer Guru appearing in a golden glow above your beer as you meditate. He will act as your personal guide and you will then find yourself astral-travelling with him, along the Beer Leys, to his cave, high in the Himalayas.

The Beer Guru's cave is sparsely furnished, as you would expect of a holy man. Just a sacred beer circle, beer altar, fridge, TV, DVD, Sony Playstation, dartboard, snooker table, bed, a Star Wars chess set and a Lord of the Rings Monopoly set.

The Beer Guru will invite you to sit with him in his sacred beer circle while he teaches you the secrets of life, beer and everything.

Keep a small notepad handy to write it all down because you may not remember everything when you return to everyday consciousness. The Beer Guru will test you when you least expect it.

Do not play him at darts or snooker for money. How do you think he got the TV, Playstation, DVD and stuff?

When the Beer Guru deems you ready, he will show you the secret entrance to the Monastery of the Beer Brothers at the back of his cave.

He can also tell you the secret of happiness.

"The secret of happiness is to drink beer and never try to teach a pig to sing."

The Beer Guru

"In Tibet, temples are called stupas. Most of the Beer Brothers are in a stupa all day long."

The Beer Guru

31

The Dalai Llager and the Monastery of the Beer Brothers

At the rear of the Beer Guru's cave is a huge golden statue of the Beer Bhudda. He is sitting in the lotus position holding a pint glass of the Golden One, Shangri-La-La-Lager.

Though all statues of all Bhuddas bear a similarity, you can always recognise the Beer Bhudda from two distinctive features. He is the only one holding a beer and the only one wearing a vest.

You will never see the Beer Bhudda with a six pack. Like most Bhuddas, he's a chubby figure with, what we would call in the western world, a bit of a beer belly. Some say that this accounts for his smile.

His face is lit with a beaming smile that radiates love and serenity. A smile that says he has achieved ecstasy, the union with the source of all happiness.

If you were to put your finger in the statue's belly button, you would find that the Beer Bhudda slides sideways revealing a secret passage. It leads to the Monastery of the Beer Brothers, who serve the Beer Goddess and look after the Font of All Wisdom.

The monastery has never been visited physically by anyone from the outside world. The Beer Guru is the only person who has ever been allowed to pass beyond this point in recent centuries. Everyone else has to travel there astrally, like you.

The long passageway is lined with smaller golden statues of the Beer Bhudda. The air is heavy with incense and the sound of monks chanting and praying.

In the distance you will hear the rattle of prayer wheels, the hum of singing bowls, the sound of gongs and bells.

Eventually, you will be led to the Beer Temple where the Dalai Llager sits in constant meditation before a huge golden glass containing 144,000 gallons of pure Light Ale.

If the Dalai Llager approves of you, he will give you a blessing and welcome you into the Beer Brotherhood.

He may also give you a spiritually symbolic gift, a saffron robe, a golden bottle opener and a new name for use only as a member of the Beer Brotherhood.

As a member of the Beer Brotherhood, the Beer Buddha, Dalai Llager and Beer Brothers can now act as your spiritual helpers and teachers on the etheric planes, just as the Beer Guru can.

You may summon them or visit them for advice and guidance whenever you wish.

"Wasssuuup. I'm having a beer with my Beer Bro buddies."

The Beer Guru

The Beer Guru is still your personal teacher. He embodies all knowledge and wisdom pertaining to sacred beer. He also possesses the Beer Bible, from which he will have already taught you many things in your visits to his cave..

You do not become a member of the Beer Brotherhood overnight. It may take days, weeks, months or years of meditation, before you are accepted and guided on the inner journey down the cave's back passage to meet the Beer Brothers and the Dalai Llager.

Stick with it. Nothing succeeds like persistence.

Do not attempt to make the journey to the Beer Brothers Monastery in the real world. You will not succeed.

There is no physical path. Only the path of the Beer Guru.

"One sip totally clears the mind of unwanted trivia."

The Beer Guru

32

The Beer Mat of the Holy Ale

You have now reached the final stages of the Beer Guru's quest. If the Beer Guru deems you worthy to continue he will appear to you in a dream and lead you to a small, ornate casket kept behind the altar in the Monastery's Beer Temple.

This casket contains one of the most important sacred relics of Shangri-La-La.

Some say it is more powerful than the Holy Grail, but it is not a chalice, or a cup. They are mere distractions for materialistic seekers of fortune.

It is the Beer Mat of the Holy Ale.

Not only is it the most sacred Holy relic of Shangri-La-La, it is the key to the final stage of the quest, the mysteries of the Beer Goddess and the Font of All Wisdom.

By all accounts, the Beer Mat of the Holy Ale looks quite unimpressive. It resembles a small brown biscuit that has been run over by a steamroller in a muddy puddle.

Appearance is no measure of spiritual power. According to legend, those who touch it will first see a vision of the Holy Ale, then one of the Beer Goddess herself, Kylie, the Universal Provider

Witnesses to this phenomenon maintain that those who are allowed to touch the Beer Mat of the Holy Ale disappear instantly in a flash of blinding light.

This has given rise to a fear that when a mortal first sees Shangri-La-La-Lager, the Golden One, they are overwhelmed by its power and majesty and die of sheer joy.

"Behold, the Beer of Glory, the Golden One.

Such is its power, grown men weep when they see it,

Then, die of delight and, on a wave of deepest joy,

are immediately transported to heaven to live

amongst the immortals for eternity. "

A Shangri-La-La legend

What really happens is that they are transported miraculously to the hidden Temple of the Beer Goddess, where will they be allowed to achieve their quest and drink from the Font of All wisdom.

There is no way you can initiate this stage of the quest yourself.

148

Only those who have studied at the Beer Guru's feet for many years will have evolved into higher spiritual beings and be accorded the honour of experiencing the ultimate truths of the Beer Guru's path.

"Beer makes the sitar sound like music."

The Beer Guru

33

The Temple of the Beer Goddess

Despite this elitist attitude, all are encouraged to attempt to achieve this level of spiritual advancement on the path of the Beer Guru.

It will, of course, be up to the Beer Guru whether you are allowed to touch the sacred Beer Mat of the Holy Ale and to be transported to the Temple of the Beer Goddess.

This is probably the greatest of the Beer Guru's mysteries, but we do know a little about the Temple of the Beer Goddess from the chosen few who have passed through its hallowed portals at this stage of their spiritual evolution and returned to tell the tale.

By all accounts, it is the oldest temple in the valley and was one of the ancient Beer Temples of a long-forgotten people.

Inside, are said to be many statues depicting men and women lost in the delights of drinking beer and love-making, in various positions from the Kama Sutra and the Beer Guru's equivalent, the Kama Booza.

It was a temple of Tantric beer and sex magic, a place where physical love was celebrated as a divine act of creation and beer was its holy libation.

The inner sanctum of the temple is circular and surrounded by statues of the nine beer muses, which are startlingly realistic.

They look like nine, real, naked woman standing on pedestals, all blessed with stunning bodies. The Beer Guru says it reminds him very much of Spearmint Rhino, another Temple of the Goddess that he regularly frequents.

The beer muses face towards the focal point of the temple, a circular altar bedecked with many pints of shimmering golden ale, all in different mugs, glasses, tankards, chalices, goblets and glasses.

One of them contains the Gold of the Gods, Shangri-La-La Lager, the elixir of life. But it will not be easy to find. It is not a whole pint, just three drops of the divine nectar in a pint of otherwise normal beer.

It will be the seeker's task to detect it.

Pick the wrong one and you will die horribly. The temple will collapse around your ears. Don't ask me why. That's just the way it is with ancient temples and mystical adventures.

While massive blocks of rock are crashing down around you, the Beer Goddesses' evil twin, Randi, will materialise, sit on your face and everything will go black as you are cast into the whirling pit of no return.

There you will spin at thirty three and a third r.p.m. for eternity.

Pick the correct glass and events will not take this terrible turn for the worse. Be warned though, the choice will not be easy.

There are no small, plain cups for the pious, like the one Indiana Jones chose in his Holy Grail film. The container holds no clues. Nor does the beer in it. It will look just like ordinary beer.

You are on your own.

It is a test of your extra-sensory perception.

"Become a higher being. Stand on a box."

The Beer Guru

34

The Font of All Wisdom

Only a man whose heart is pure can lift the correct glass.

Select wisely and a shaft of sunlight will suddenly cut through the air from a crack in the cavernous roof hundreds of feet above, striking one of the glasses and illuminating it, so that the beer shines golden like the sun itself.

A golden glow will then spread throughout the entire temple, lighting it up like a summers' day.

A massive gold statue of the Beer Goddess will rise out of the floor in the centre of the temple and lift you into her many arms.

Do not worry that you will be crushed lifeless against her ample bosoms. You must give yourself up to her embrace. She will sink back through the floor into the Inner Sanctum of the temple, carrying you with her.

No-one has ever revealed what they found in the Inner Sanctum.

Some say it is a huge bar where you can sample hundreds of sacred beers from all over the world and never have a hangover.

Others claim that there is only one beer pump, the Font of All Wisdom, served by the Beer Goddess herself, who will manifest as the most beautiful woman you have ever seen.

As you watch her fill the beer glass with the Golden One, it will fill you with awe.

William Blake saw the world in a grain of sand. You will see the universe and eternity in a glass of beer.

Its colour will remind you of burnished gold, glinting on a summer's day. The bubbles rising through it will sparkle like stars. The head will remind you of a bright full moon on a clear night.

When you raise the glass to your lips and take a single sip, for the first time in your life, everything will make perfect sense. You will become all-knowing, all-wise.

The Beer Guru's smile will spread across your face and you will become enlightened from within.

You will become the living embodiment of the Golden One, a god amongst men.

The Beer Goddess will take you as her consort. Her nine muses will be your personal servants and will attend to your every need.

It's a tough job, but someone has to do it.

"If you have a beer in your hand
you will have love in your heart
and a smile on your face."

The Beer Guru

35

The Secret of the Beer Guru's Smile

Now you have drunk from the Font of All Wisdom, your path of enlightenment is at an end. You stand empowered as a Beer Guru in your own right.

The evidence will be written all over your face in the shape of the Beer Guru's knowing smile which you will now have acquired.

It is called a knowing smile because it is the knowledge you now hold that makes a new Beer Guru smile.

It is knowledge that fills you full of joy, happiness and love of life.

It is the smile of one who knows bliss.

It is the smile of one who knows the secret of life.

It is the smile of one whose veins run with beer.

It is the smile of one whose head is a froth of new knowledge and ideas.

Remarkably, you do not have to drink from the Font of All Wisdom to acquire a smile like this.

You can catch it, as you would catch a cold.

Smiles are highly contagious and spread swiftly from face to face, from person to person.

Merely looking at a picture of the Beer Guru or a statue of the Beer Bhudda can cause their smile to spread to your face.

As will performing your Beer Guru exercises, drinking the sacred beer and drawing on the secret powers of beer.

All can fit your face with a massive, beneficent grin.

Be aware that it is a smile that holds secrets. As soon as you acquire it, it will begin to release some of those secrets to you.

Try it. Smile like the Beer Guru and you will find that you feel different almost immediately.

You can actually feel energy spreading from the smile into your face, your heart, your soul and the rest of your being.

How this happens is one of the Beer Guru's mysteries, but it definitely does happen and you will feel it for yourself.

When you have experienced the power of the Beer Guru's smile, you will understand why it is probably the most important thing the Beer Guru could give you.

"If you have a beer in your hand, you will have love in your heart and a smile on your face."

The Beer Guru

If you have persevered with all the Beer Guru's teachings, I thank you and bless you for your attention and patience.

You have come a long way and will certainly have been transformed by the experience. Remember what you have learnt, what your eyes have seen and your ears heard.

If you have touched the Beer Mat of the Holy Ale and become one with the Beer Goddess, you are now truly a Beer Guru yourself.

You will have been blessed with all the mystical powers of beer listed in Chapter 28.

You will also have discovered that, ironically, once you have achieved the status of Beer Guru and attained union with your higher self, you are above all that.

You will then understand why the most important lesson of the Beer Guru's teachings, is to put a smile on your face.

"You will then realise that the truly enlightened do not need a beer or anything else to be who they really are."

The Beer Guru

CLOUD NINE

"At the end of the beer guru's
spiritual path, you will be
completely blissed up."

The Beer Guru